Simon Steph[...]

Pornography

Simon
Stephens

Methuen Drama

Published by Methuen Drama 2008

3 5 7 9 10 8 6 4

Methuen Drama
A & C Black Publishers Limited
36 Soho Square
London W1D 3QY
www.acblack.com

ISBN 978 1 408 11056 0

A CIP catalogue record for this book is available from
the British Library

Typeset by Country Setting, Kingsdown, Kent
Printed and bound in Great Britain by
CPI Cox & Wyman Ltd, Reading, Berkshire

TRAVERSE THEATRE
SCOTLAND'S NEW WRITING THEATRE

THE REP
Birmingham Repertory Theatre

Traverse Theatre Company & Birmingham Repertory Theatre Company

Pornography
By Simon Stephens

Cast in alphabetical order

Frances Ashman
Loo Brealey
Sacha Dhawan
Amanda Hale
Jeff Rawle
Sheila Reid
Billy Seymour
Sam Spruell

Director	Sean Holmes
Designer	Paul Wills
Lighting Designer	Chris Davey
Sound Designer	Emma Laxton
Casting Director	Amy Ball

Stage Manager	Graham Michael
Deputy Stage Manager	Danni Bastian
Assistant Stage Manager	Gabriel Bartlett

First performed at the Traverse Theatre
Monday 28 July 2008

Pornography was commissioned and originally produced by
Deutsches Schauspielhaus, Hamburg.

Company Biographies

Frances Ashman

Frances trained at Guildhall School of Music and Drama. Theatre credits include *Macbeth*, *Pericles*, *The Winter's Tale* (Royal Shakespeare Company). Television credits include *Gunrush* (ITV productions), *Trial and Retribution* (La Plante Productions). Film credits include *Nil By Mouth* (SE8 Productions). Frances has been lead singer in various bands including The Circle and The Egg. She also wrote and performed two tracks for the soundtrack of *Nil By Mouth*.

Loo Brealey

Loo trained at Cambridge University and Ecole Philippe Gaulier, London. Theatre credits include Sonya in *Uncle Vanya* (English Touring Theatre, Dir - Sir Peter Hall); Nell in *Little Nell* (Theatre Royal, Bath, Dir - Sir Peter Hall); *After the End* (Paines Plough); *Arcadia* (Bristol Old Vic/Birmingham Repertory Theatre); *Sliding With Suzanne* (Royal Court Theatre). Television credits include: *Hotel Babylon* (Carnival); *Green* (Granada); *Bleak House, Mayo* and two series of *Casualty* as Roxy. Radio credits include: *The Ring and the Book, Have Your Cake* (BBC Radio 4); *I Will Tell* (Catherine Bailey Productions/BBC Radio 4).

Chris Davey (Lighting Designer)

For the Royal National Theatre: *Harper Regan, The Seagull, The Pillars of the Community, A Dream Play, Iphiginia at Aulis, War and Peace, Baby Doll, The Colour of Justice*. For the RSC: *Twelfth Night, The Winter's Tale, Pericles, Cymbeline, Alice in Wonderland, Night of the Soul, Romeo and Juliet, A Midsummer Night's Dream, Everyman* (both also in New York), *A Month in the Country, Troilus and Cressida, The Comedy of Errors* (world tour) *Mysteria, Easter*. Chris has also designed extensively for Shared Experience Theatre, Hampstead Theatre, Royal Exchange Manchester, West Yorkshire Playhouse, Royal Lyceum Edinburgh and Birmingham Rep. Other designs include: *Hay Fever* (Royal Exchange Manchester); *War and Peace* (Shared Experience/Hampstead) *Matthew Bourne's The Car Man* (Sadler's Wells/Old Vic and national tour); *The Pianist* (Manchester International Festival); *Peer Gynt* (Dundee Rep/National Theatre of Scotland); *One Flew Over the Cuckoo's Nest* (Garrick/Geilgud Theatres and national tour); *Don't Look Now* (Sheffield Lyceum/Lyric Hammersmith); *Catch, The Sugar Syndrome, Crazyblackmuthafuckinself, The Force of Change* (Royal Court Theatre); *Three Thousand Troubled Threads* (Stellar Quines/Edinburgh International Festival); *Watership Down, The Odyssey, The Magic Carpet, Then Again, Cause Celebre* (Lyric Hammersmith); *The Earthly Paradise* (Almeida Theatre); *Yellowman* (Liverpool/Hampstead); *The Odyssey, Beasts and Beauties* (Bristol Old Vic); *21* (Rambert Dance Company); *Jekyll and Hyde* (Northern Ballet Theatre); *Shining Souls* (Old Vic); *In a Little World of Our Own, Endgame* (Donmar Warehouse); *Blood Wedding, Grimm Tales* (Young Vic). Opera include: *Aida* (Houston Grand Opera); *The Rake's Progress* (Aldeburgh Festival); *Bluebeard* (Bregenz & St Polten); *Jephtha* (English National Opera/Welsh National Opera); *The Magic Flute* (Welsh National Opera); eight seasons at Grange Park Opera, *The Picture of Dorian Gray* (Opera de Monte Carlo).

Sacha Dhawan

Sacha played the role of Akthar in the original award winning production of *The History Boys* by Alan Bennett (Royal National Theatre). He later reprised the role for the Broadway production, the international tour and the film adaptation. Other theatre work includes: *Free Outgoing, Monkery* (Royal Court Theatre); *Pretend You Have Big Buildings* (Royal Exchange Theatre); *Borstal Boy* (Edinburgh Festival Fringe 2007); *Skater Boy* (Theatre Royal Stratford East); *The Witches, East is East* (Leicester Haymarket Theatre). He recently won Breakthrough On-Screen at the Royal Television Society Awards for his performance in the controversial drama *Bradford Riots*. Other television credits include: *Wired, Perfectly Frank, Weirdsister College, Altogether Now, City Central, The Last Train* and *Out of Sight*. Radio credits include *Bollywood Jane, The Interpreter, Takeaway: 1979, The Prospect, Excluded, The History Boys, Silver Street, Westway* and *Chocky*. Film credits include: *Splintered*, which is set for release in 2008.

Amanda Hale

Amanda trained at RADA and recently starred in Katie Mitchell's *The City* at the Royal Court Theatre. Other recent projects include *The Glass Menagerie* (Bill Kenwright Productions/The Lyric) for which she was nominated Most Outstanding Newcomer 2007 for The Evening Standard Milton Shulman Award. She was also nominated for Most Promising Newcomer for The Critics Circle Awards 2005 for *Crooked* at the Bush Theatre. Television credits include: *Persuasion* (ITV), *Richard is My Boyfriend* (Windfall Films/Channel Four). Amanda has just completed filming on Jane Campion's film *Bright Star*.

Sean Holmes (Director)

Sean was Associate Director at Oxford Stage Company from 2001 - 2006. Directing credits include *The English Game* (Yvonne Arnaud Theatre, Guildford); *The Man Who Had All the Luck* (Donmar Warehouse); *Moonlight and Magnolias*, *Singer*, *The Price* (Tricycle Theatre); *The Entertainer* (Old Vic Theatre); *Caucasian Chalk Circle* (Royal National Theatre/Filter Theatre Company); *Julius Caesar*, *A New Way to Please You*, *Richard III*, *Measure for Measure*, *Roman Actor* (Royal Shakespeare Company); *Cleansed*, *Home*, *The Comedians*, *The Contractor* (Oxford Stage Company); *Translations*, *The Mentalists*, *A Midsummer Night's Dream* (Royal National Theatre); *Incomplete and Random Acts of Kindness* (Royal Court Theatre); *The Price* (Apollo Theatre).

Emma Laxton (Sound Designer)

West End theatre credits include: *That Face* (Duke of York's); *My Name Is Rachel Corrie* (Playhouse Theatre). Other theatre includes *2000 Feet Away*, *Tinderbox* (The Bush Theatre); *Shoot/Get Treasure/Repeat* (Royal National Theatre); *Europe* (Dundee Rep/Barbican Pit); *Other Hands* (Soho Theatre); *The Unthinkable* (Sheffield Theatres); *My Dad is a Birdman* (Young Vic); *The Gods Are Not To Blame* (Arcola Theatre) and *Late Fragment* (Tristan Bates Theatre). For The Royal Court Theatre: *That Face*, *Gone Too Far!*, *Catch*, *Scenes From The Back of Beyond*, *Woman and Scarecrow*, *The World's Biggest Diamond*, *Incomplete And Random Acts of Kindness*, *My Name Is Rachel Corrie* (also Minetta Lane, New York/Galway Festival/Edinburgh Festival Fringe), *Bone*, *The Weather*, *Bear Hug*, *Terrorism*, *Food Chain*.

Jeff Rawle

Theatre credits include: *Fram*, *Noises Off* (Royal National Theatre); *King of Hearts* (Hampstead Theatre/Out of Joint); *Bottle Universe* (Bush Theatre); *Way to Heaven*, *The Arbor*, *Bent* (Royal Court Theatre); *Neville's Island*, *Queerfolk* (Nottingham Playhouse); *Releevo*, *Living With Your Enemies* (Soho Theatre); *Reluctant Heroes*, *The Elephant Man* (Churchill, Bromley); *Butley* (Fortune Theatre); *The Anniversary* (Liverpool Playhouse); *Once a Catholic* (Wyndham's Theatre); *Equus* (Aldwych Theatre); *Five Finger Exercise* (Upstream Theatre). Television credits include: George in six series of *Drop the Dead Donkey* (Channel 4); three series of *Doc Martin* (ITV); Billy Liar in *Billy Liar* (LWT); *New Tricks*, *Fear Stress and Anger*, *The Lightening Kid*, *The Last Detective*, *Sea of Souls*, *Spooks*, *A Touch of Frost*, *Ultimate Force*, *My Dad's the Prime Minister*, *William and Mary*, *Bedtime*, *The Deputy*, *Death in Holy Orders*, *Dalziel and Pascoe*, *Take A Girl Like You*, *I Saw You*, *Fish*, *Microsoap*, *Neville's Island*, *Faith in the Future*, *Sharman*, *Blood and Peaches*, *Lords of Misrule*, *Look at the State We're in Chief*, *The Life and Times of Henry Pratt*, *Medics*, *Minder*, *Wycliffe*, *Rides*, *A Perfect Hero*, *The Gift*, *Vote for Them*, *South of the Border*, *Run for the Lifeboat*, *Boon*, *Fortunes of War*, *Call Me Mister*, *Remmington Steel*, *Country and Irish*, *Dr Who*, *Singles Weekend*, *Bergerac*, *Claire*, *Juliet Bravo*, *Singles*, *Wilde Alliance*, *Love on the Dole*, *Death of a Young Young Man*, *The Water Maiden*. Film credits include: *Harry Potter and the Goblet of Fire*, *Blackball*, *Inspector Calls Too*, *The Life Story of Baal*, *A Hitch in Time*, *Correction Please*, *Rating Notman*, *Duchamp*, *Crystal Gazing*, *Awayday*, *Laughterhouse*, *Doctors and the Devils*.

Sheila Reid

Theatre credits include: *In Extremis* (Shakespeare's Globe); *Girl With Red Hair* (Royal Lyceum Theatre/Bush Theatre); *Dona Rosita* (The Orange Tree); *Richard III*, *Romeo and Juliet*, *Virtuoso*, *'Tis Pity She's A Whore*, *King Baby* (Royal Shakespeare Company); *Terrorism*, *Black Milk*, *My Mother Said I Never Should*, *Short Change*, *The Gentle Avalanche* (Royal Court Theatre); *The Circle* (Oxford Stage Company); *Abandonment* (Traverse Theatre); *One Flea Spare*, *The Marshelling Yard*, *When I Was A Girl I Used To Scream And Shout* (Bush Theatre/Whitehall - Olivier Nomination); *Tartuffe*, *King Lear*, *The Wood Demon* (Actors Company - founder member); *The Good Hope*, *The Crucible*, *Hedda Gabler*, *Three Sisters*, *Othello*, *Beaux Stratagem*, *Love's Labours Lost* (Royal National Theatre); *The Winter Guest* (West Yorkshire Playhouse/Almeida and on film). Musical theatre credits include: *Sweeney Todd* (Royal National Theatre); *Martin Guerre* (Prince Edward); *Into The Woods* (Donmar Warehouse). Television credits include: *Bones* (20th Century Fox); *Place of Execution*, *A Room With A View*, Madge in two series of *Benidorm* (ITV); *What We Did On Our Holidays*, *Your Mother Should Know*, *Sea of Souls*, *Casualty*, *Monarch of the Glen*, *Doctor Who*, *Auf Wiedersen Pet* (BBC); *A Christmas Carol* (Hallmark), *Dr Finlay*, *Taggart* (STV); *Where The Heart Is* (Anglia). Radio credits include: *Villette* directed by John Dove. Film credits include: *Hush*, *One Careful Owner*, *Home Grown*, *The Touch*, *Sir Henry At Rawlinsons End*, *Felicia's Journey*, *Mrs Caldicott's Cabbage War*, *American Friends*, *Brazil*.

Billy Seymour

Theatre credits include *Pretend You Have Big Buildings* (Royal Exchange Theatre); *Christmas* (Bush Theatre); *Sing Yer Heart Out for the Lads* (Royal National Theatre); *Herons* (Royal Court Theatre). Television credits include *The Odditorium* (Celador Productions Ltd); *GI Jonny, Ruby in the Smoke, Brainfood, The Canterbury Tales, The Pig Heart Boy* (BBC); *The Bill* (ITV); *Bella and the Boys* (Century Films); *Brussels* (Channel 4). Film credits include *Atonement* (Tallis Pictures Ltd); *Hot Fuzz* (Town Square Films); *Chromophobia* (Optimum); *Mrs Henderson Presents* (The Weinstein Company); *Vera Drake* (Fine Line Features); *Ted and Sylvia* (Focus Features); *A Christmas Carol* (Hallmark).

Sam Spruell

Theatre credits include *The Alchemist, Life of Galileo* (Royal National Theatre); *Lear* (Sheffield Crucible); *Othello* (Royal Exchange Theatre); *A Midsummer Night's Dream, They Shoot Horses, Don't They?, Pipin* (Bloomsbury Theatre); *Biloxi Blues* (Arts Theatre). Television credits include *Spooks, Holby Blue, Silent Witness* (BBC); *City of Vice* (Touchpaper Television); *Ghost Squad, POW* (Company Pictures). Film credits include *Defiance* (GHM Films); *Elizabeth: The Golden Age* (Working Title); *Venus, To Kill a King* (Film Four); *London to Brighton* (Steel Mill); *K19 The Widowmaker, The Hurtlocker, The Dreamer, The Sleeping Dictionary* (First Light Productions).

Simon Stephens (Writer)

Simon Stephens plays include *Harper Regan* (2008, Royal National Theatre); *Pornography* (2007, Deutsche Schauspielhaus, Hamburg); *Motortown* (2006, Royal Court Theatre); *On The Shore Of The Wide World* (2005, Royal Exchange Theatre/Royal National Theatre); *Country Music* (2004, Royal Court Theatre); *Christmas* (2003, APE/Bush Theatre); *One Minute* (2003, ATC/Sheffield Theatres/Bush Theatre); *Port* (2002, Royal Exchange); *Herons* (2001, Royal Court Theatre); *Bluebird* (1998, Royal Court Theatre). Several of his plays have been performed throughout Europe, the US and Australia. He was awarded the Pearson Award for Best Play for *Port* in 2002. *On The Shore Of The Wide World* won Best New Play for 2005 at the Manchester Evening News Awards and the Olivier Award for Best New Play in 2006. *Motortown* won best International Play in Theater Heute, Germany in 2007. *Pornography* was invited to the Berlin Theater Treffen in 2008. Simon was the resident dramatist at the Royal Court Theatre in 2000 and he was the Writers Tutor at the Royal Court Young Writers Programme between 2001 - 2005. He was the Pearson attached playwright at the Royal Exchange in 2001 and in 2006 he was the first ever Resident Dramatist at the National Theatre.

Paul Wills (Designer)

Paul's recent design credits include: *The Man Who Had All the Luck* (Donmar Warehouse); *Testing the Echo* (Out of Joint/Tour); *The Frontline* (Shakespeare's Globe); *See How They Run* (Royal Exchange Theatre); *Rusalka* (English Touring Opera); *Inparenthesis* and *Overspill* in the *Metamorphosis 08* Project at the Churchill Theatre, Bromley with ATG. He was designer on *Prometheus Bound*, recently remounted at the Classic Stage Company in New York (and previously at Sound) and other work includes *The Changeling* (set, English Touring Theatre); *Crestfall* (Theatre 503); *We the People* (Shakespeare's Globe); *Tracy Beaker Gets Real* (Nottingham Playhouse/UK tour); *The Cut* (Donmar Warehouse/Tour, TMA Award for Best Touring production); *Invisible Mountains* (Royal National Theatre); *Little Voice* (Watermill Theatre); *Sleeping Beauty* (Helix Theatre, Dublin); *Total Eclipse* (set, Menier Chocolate Factory); *A Model Girl*, a new musical about the Profumo Affair (Greenwich); *A Number* (Sheffield Crucible Studio & Chichester Festival); *Mother Courage* (set, English Touring Theatre); *The Field* (Tricycle Theatre); *Gladiator Games* (Sheffield Crucible/Theatre Royal Stratford East); *Mammals* (Bush Theatre/Tour); *Blue/Orange* (Sheffield Theatre/Tour) and *Breathing Corpses* (Royal Court Theatre). He also designed *Sweetness and Badness* for Welsh National Opera's *Max* project and *The Magic Flute* directed by Sam West at the National Theatre of Palestine, Bethlehem and Ramallah.

The Traverse

Artistic Director Dominic Hill

The importance of the Traverse is difficult to overestimate... without the theatre, it is difficult to imagine Scottish playwriting at all. (SUNDAY TIMES)
The Traverse's commissioning process embraces a spirit of innovation and risk-taking that has launched the careers of many of Scotland's best-known writers including John Byrne, David Greig, David Harrower and Liz Lochhead. It is unique in Scotland in that it fulfils the crucial role of providing the infrastructure, professional support and expertise to ensure the development of a dynamic theatre culture for Scotland.

The Traverse Theatre, the festival's most prestigious home of serious drama. (NEW YORK TIMES)
From its conception in the 1960s, the Traverse has remained a pivotal venue in Edinburgh. It receives enormous critical and audience acclaim for its programming, as well as regularly winning awards. Most recently, Alan Wilkins' commission for the Traverse, *Carthage Must Be Destroyed*, won Best New Play at the 2008 Critics' Awards for Theatre in Scotland. From 2001 - 07, Traverse productions of *Gagarin Way* by Gregory Burke, *Outlying Islands* by David Greig, *Iron* by Rona Munro, *The People Next Door* by Henry Adam, *Shimmer* by Linda McLean, *When the Bulbul Stopped Singing* by Raja Shehadeh, *East Coast Chicken Supper* by Martin J Taylor, *Strawberries in January* by Evelyne de la Chenelière in a version by Rona Munro and *Damascus* by David Greig have won Fringe First or Herald Angel awards (and occasionally both).

In 2007 the Traverse's Festival programme *Faithful* picked up an incredible 12 awards including Fringe Firsts for Tim Crouch's *ENGLAND* (a Traverse commission) and the Traverse Theatre production of *Damascus* by David Greig, plus a Herald Archangel for outgoing Artistic Director Philip Howard for "his consistent and lasting contribution to Edinburgh's Festivals".

A Rolls-Royce machine for promoting new Scottish drama across Europe and beyond. (THE SCOTSMAN)
The Traverse's success isn't limited to the Edinburgh stage. Since 2001 Traverse productions of *Gagarin Way*, *Outlying Islands*, *Iron*, *The People Next Door*, *When the Bulbul Stopped Singing*, the *Slab Boys Trilogy*, *Mr Placebo* and *Helmet* have toured not only within Scotland and the UK, but in Sweden, Norway, the Balkans, Germany, USA, Iran, Jordan and Canada. Immediately following the 2006 festival, the Traverse's production of *Petrol Jesus Nightmare #5 (In the Time of the Messiah)* by Henry Adam was invited to perform at the International Festival in Priština, Kosovo and won the Jury Special Award for Production. During Spring 2008, the Traverse toured its award winning 2007 production of *Damascus* to Toronto, New York and Moscow.

Discover more about the Traverse at www.traverse.co.uk

Traverse Theatre - The Company

Katy Brignall	Assistant Box Office Manager
Andy Catlin	Marketing Manager
Laura Collier	Associate Producer
Maureen Deacon	Finance Assistant
Steven Dickson	Head Chef
Neil Donachie	Bar Café Duty Manager
Martin Duffield	Box Office Manager
Claire Elliot	Assistant Electrician
Craig Fyfe	Commis Chef
Mike Griffiths	Administrative Director
Gavin Harding	Production Manager
Dominic Hill	Artistic Director
Sarah Holland	Wardrobe Supervisor
Aimee Johnstone	Bar Café Assistant Manager
Kath Lowe	Front of House Manager
Norman Macleod	Development Manager
Euan McLaren	Deputy Electrician
Katherine Mendelsohn	Literary Manager
Sarah Murray	Administrative Assistant
Noelle O'Donoghue	Learning & Participation Officer
Gwen Orr	Theatre Manager
Emma Pirie	Press & Marketing Officer
Pauleen Rafferty	Finance & Personnel Assistant
Renny Robertson	Chief Electrician
Steven Simpson	Executive Bar Café Manager
Laura Sinton	Temporary Development Assistant
Lindsey Smith	Finance Manager
Louise Stephens	Literary Assistant
Phil Turner	Technical Stage Manager
Liz Wallace	Marketing & Press Assistant
Alan Wilkins	Young Writers Group Leader

Also working for the Traverse Peter Airlie, Liam Boucher, Peter Boyd, Hannah Cornish, Michael Craik, Koralia Daskalaki, Oliver Dimelow, Morag Donnachie, Marianne Forde, Andrew Gannon, Ernest Graham, Linda Gunn, Zophie Horsted, Adam James, Neil Johnstone, Tessa Kelly, Rebecca King, Anna Kulikowska, Terry Leddy, Kate Leiper, Graeme Mackie, Heather Marshall, Alan Massie, Jon-James McGregor, Helen McIntosh, Lynn Middleton, John Mitchell, Ewa Nagraba, Grant Neave, Christie O'Carroll, Niamh O'Meara, Matthew Ozga-Lawn, Clare Padgett, Laura Penny, Tim Primrose, Michael Ramsay, Emma Robertson, Greg Sinclair, Caitlin Skinner, David Taylor, Emma Taylor, Kate Temple, Naomi Turner, James Turner Inman, Anna Walsh, Jenna Watt, Katie Wilson.

TRAVERSE THEATRE BOARD OF DIRECTORS
Stewart Binnie, Stephen Cotton (Chair), Adrienne Sinclair Chalmers (Company Secretary), Lynne Crossan, Susan Deacon, Caroline Gardner, David Greig, Chris Hannan, Sheila Murray, Margaret Waterston.

Traverse Theatre Sponsorship & Development

We would like to thank the following corporate funders for their support:

To find out how you can benefit from being a Traverse Corporate Funder, please contact our Development Department on 0131 228 3223 / development@traverse.co.uk.

The Traverse would like to thank the members of the Development Board:
Stewart Binnie, Adrienne Sinclair Chalmers, Stephen Cotton, Paddy Scott and Ian Wittet

The Traverse Theatre's work would not be possible without the support of

BRITISH COUNCIL   ·EDINBVRGH· THE CITY OF EDINBURGH COUNCIL   Scottish **Arts** Council

The Traverse Theatre receives financial assistance from:

The Barcapel Foundation, The Binks Trust, The Calouste Gulbenkian Foundation,
The Canadian High Commission, The Craignish Trust, The Cross Trust, The Cruden Foundation,
Gouvernement de Québec, James Thom Howat Charitable Trust, The Japan Foundation,
The John Thaw Foundation, The Lloyds TSB Foundation for Scotland, The Misses Barrie Charitable Trust,
The Moffat Charitable Trust, The Peggy Ramsay Foundation, Ronald Duncan Literary Foundation,
Sky Youth Action Fund, Tay Charitable Trust, The Thistle Trust, The Weatherall Foundation

Charity No. SC002368

Our Devotees Joan Aitken, Stewart Binnie, Katie Bradford, Adrienne Sinclair Chalmers, Adam Fowler,
Joscelyn Fox, Anne Gallacher, Keith Guy, John Knight OBE, Iain Millar, Gillian Moulton, Helen Pitkethly,
Michael Ridings, Bridget Stevens, Walton & Parkinson.

For their continued generous support of Traverse productions, the Traverse thanks:
The Pier, 104 George Street, Edinburgh; Habitat; Camerabase

Birmingham Repertory Theatre Company

Birmingham Repertory Theatre is one of Britain's leading national producing theatre companies. From its base in Birmingham, The REP produces over 20 new productions each year.

The commissioning and production of new work lies at the core of The REP's programme. The Door was established ten years ago as a theatre dedicated to the production and presentation of new writing. In this time, it has given world premieres to new plays from a new generation of British playwrights. The REP itself received The Peggy Ramsay Award for New Writing, enabling us to develop and commission more new plays for the future.

Developing new and particularly younger audiences is also at the heart of The REP's work, in its various Education initiatives, such as Transmissions, The Young REP, REP's Children, as well as with the programming of work in The Door for children.

The REP's productions regularly transfer to London and tour nationally and internationally. Recent transfers and tours have included *Brief Encounter, She Stoops To Conquer, Taking Care Of Baby, Glorious!, The Birthday Party, The Witches, Through The Woods, Of Mice And Men, A Doll's House, The Crucible, Celestina, Hamlet, The Ugly Eagle, The Old Masters, The Snowman, The Gift, Behsharam (Shameless)* and *The Ramayana*.

Artistic Director Rachel Kavanaugh
Executive Director Stuart Rogers
Associate Director (Literary) Ben Payne

Book online at birmingham-rep.co.uk.

Birmingham Repertory Theatre is a registered charity, number 223660

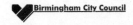

Birmingham Repertory Theatre Company

Join The REP Club

Come here often?
Want to receive generous savings, special offers, priority booking and invites to special events?
Ever wanted to know more about the show you've come to see or to ask an actor a question?

The REP Club gets invites to talks with members of The REP's creative teams.

Annual benefits of membership include:
• A free backstage tour
• Discounted tickets and priority booking
• Free cloakroom usage and four free programmes
• Press Nights for just £10 in the Main House and £5 in The Door when booked together
• Regular invitations to special Offstage LIVE events
• Up to date backstage information and the latest news

Cost £50 per year.

For more information visit birmingham-rep.co.uk or call the Box Office on 0121 236 4455.

With thanks to:

Corporate Sponsors

Supporters:

Pornography

Pornography was originally translated into German by Barbara Christ and was first presented in a co-production between the Deutschen Schauspielhauses, Hamburg, and the Festival Theaterformen and the Schauspielhannover in Hanover. It received its world premiere in Hanover on 15 June 2007 and transferred to Hamburg on 5 October 2007. The cast was as follows:

Sonja Beisswenger
Christoph Franken
Peter Knaack
Angela Muethel
Jana Schulz
Monique Schwitter
Daniel Wahl
Samuel Weiss

Director Sebastian Nübling
Designer Muriel Gerstner
Lighting Roland Edrich
Music Lars Wittershagen
Costume designer Marion Münch
Dramaturgs Nicola Bramkamp, Regina Guhl, David Tushingham

This play can be performed by any number of actors.
It can be performed in any order.

I am going to keep this short and to the point, because it's all been said before by far more eloquent people than me.

But our words have no impact upon you, therefore I'm going to talk to you in a language that you understand. Our words are dead until we give them life with our blood.

Images of hell.
They are silent.

What you need to do is stand well clear of the yellow line.

Images of hell.
They are silent.

Seven

I wake up and I think he's drowning. I can hear the sound of him in his cot. His breath is tight and he's gasping. I go into his room. Stand there. Every bone is as small as a finger. He's not drowning. Of course he's not drowning, he's on dry land. It's Saturday morning. He's still asleep. I watch his chest rise and fall. It would take only the lightest of forces from an adult's arm to crush the bones in his ribcage. I feel so much love for him that my heart fills up. I can feel it filling up. Like a balloon.

It's six thirty.

I go back into my bedroom. I crawl under the covers. Jonathan, my husband, is lying on his side. When I get back into the bed he lays his arm across me. It's incredibly heavy. Like it's made out of leather.

I wait for Lenny, for my son, to wake up.

He does.

I turn the radio on downstairs. I put the kettle on. I put Lenny in his chair. He's grumpy this morning. I make a pot of three cups of Jamaican Blue Mountain coffee. And slowly, methodically, I sit and drink all three cups myself.

I let Jonathan sleep.

I don't remember any news story that was on the radio that day. Apart from everybody's talking about, there's a concert. A man's talking about this concert. And exactly what it is going to achieve I must admit I find a little unclear. But he's deeply passionate about the whole affair. And the singer's passion, and Lenny's grumpiness, the little tiny whining noises that he makes, and the taste of the coffee and the feeling of wood on my table means that I find, to my surprise, that there are tears pouring down my face and falling onto the newspaper which the boy, some boy, a boy I think, at least I think it's a boy, delivered, must have delivered at some point this morning.

I go shopping in the afternoon and in my head I'm already getting prepared for work next week.

I push Lenny in his pushchair. He's got one of those three-wheeled pushchairs. It has fabulous suspension. It makes it ideal for city street life. I buy myself a pair of sandals which are pink and they have this golden strap with a little pink flower on. I think in the shops everybody's got the concert on. It's that man I like. He's singing the song about looking at the stars. Look at the stars. See how they shine for you. Maybe today is the most important day that there's ever been. And this is the biggest success of human organisation that we've ever known. And everybody should be given a knighthood of some description. There should be some kind of knighthood which is given out to all of the people there. To the people who sell the ice creams even. They should get an ice-cream seller's knighthood. For the important selling of ice cream at a time of organisational urgency. I'd like to watch the Queen knight the boys selling ice cream in Hyde Park today. She wouldn't even need to walk far from her house. She could go on a bike. It would take her five minutes. This is a day of that level of importance.

I'm pushing him so much that he falls to sleep in the end. You bump up and down. I want to walk home. I could duck south of Euston Road. I could head through Bloomsbury. Today is a day for heading through Bloomsbury with a new pair of summer sandals, ideal for the beach, on a Saturday.

I don't.

I start off.

And then I get the bus from Holborn.

And I get home and Jonathan's not there. He should be there. He should be at home. I don't have the slightest idea where he is. I try not to think about it. The house is quieter without him.

Where were you? Where were you? Which shops? What were you doing? What were you doing there? What were you buying? What are you going to paint? I want to know what you need paint for. I want to know what you want to paint. I want to know where you've been. Do you like my sandals? I bought some sandals, do you like them? I bought them for the beach. For the summer.

Sunday's Jonathan's day with Lenny. He takes him to buy newspapers. I sleep in. But Lenny starts crying when Jonathan's putting his shoes on. He's putting his shoes on wrong. His socks are bunched up over his feet. He's put his little socks on and not pulled them up properly and they're all bunched up so the shoes are uncomfortable and he starts to cry. I say to myself I am not getting up out of bed to help him. I am not getting up out of bed to help him. I am not getting up out of bed to help him.

They leave. I have no idea what I'm going to do today. I sit still for up to half an hour at a time.

I don't know where he takes him. He's windswept when he comes back. Windswept and scruffy and Lenny's crabby but happy. When Jonathan's hair is like that. When his hair is all over the place and there's a sense that he's been outside because his cheeks are all pink. I look at him and there's something about him which is enough to make me smile.

We eat our tea in front of the television when Lenny's in bed. I want Jonathan to touch me. If he were to reach out and touch me. Just rest his hand on my neck and stroke the back of my hair. If he were to do that now. Right now. Right this second.

I drop Lenny off at Julia's and he squeaks with happiness.

The tube is full of people and nearly all of them nowadays have iPods. I can't remember when that happened.

I head into work.

The Triford report is nearly finished. It's nearly ready. When it's ready. If we get it right. If David gets it right then the implications for the company are, well, they are immense. We actually did have to sign a contract that forbade us to speak even to our spouses about what was going on. It's a legally binding contract. There are rumours that Catigar Jones are working in a similar area. But David thinks they're months behind our work. Their R&D is flawed. R&D is the key to these things. David doesn't smile at me. He doesn't wish me good morning. He doesn't ask about Lenny. Or about my weekend. He asks me if I'm feeling ready. This is a big week.

I take my lunch break in Russell Square. All I ever seem to eat any more is duck hoisin wraps. I ring Julia. Lenny's fine. Everything's fine.

Jonathan doesn't ring.

At the end of the afternoon, there's a man in the square who's taken his top off and started doing press-ups. On my way back home I watch him. I watch the muscles down his spine. I watch the rivulets of sweat on the back of his neck.

At home, I am very tempted to explain to Jonathan exactly about the Triford report. To tell him in complete detail about the nature of the report. Explain it to him meticulously. Encourage him to sell the details to Catigar Jones.

He's watching the news. There's been another car bomb in a market in Baghdad. There's always a car bomb in a market in

Baghdad. I don't watch. I try to read my magazine. I'd rather watch *Sex and the City*. *Sex and the City* is on. Can we watch *Sex and the City*, please?

I want to go on a long-haul flight. I'd like to take Lenny on a long-haul flight. I like the screens, the in-flight maps on the backs of the seats in front of you. They allow you to trace the arc of the flight. They allow you to see the size of the world. They allow you to imagine the various war zones that you're flying over. You're flying over war zones. You're flying over Iraq. You're flying over Iran. You're flying over Afghanistan. And Turkmenistan. And Kazakhstan. And Chechnya. On your long-haul flight. On your way out on holiday. With the sandals that you bought with the gold strap and the plastic pink flower.

When Lenny sleeps he sticks him bum in the air. He sleeps on his knees. He wraps his blanket around himself. He's incredibly sweaty. It's Monday night and I get up again and get out of bed to check he's all right. Jonathan doesn't notice I've gone. I lie down on the floor next to his cot. Watch him breathe. Fall asleep on his floor. I go back to bed at about five o'clock and can't sleep. What did he want to buy paint for? Where did he go to buy his paint?

In the morning I can't decipher all of the different news stories on the radio.

Jonathan comes downstairs in a suit and he's so clean. His hair is clean. And his skin. He's had a shave. He grabs a banana and runs out of the door.

The freezer needs defrosting. There's a crust of ice that sits on everything. It takes a while to open the drawer and chip away at the cubes. They always make the same sound when you drop them in the glass. And their frost is settled by the whisky. My hand is shaking. It's eight in the morning. It's Tuesday. It feels fucking amazing.

I manage to get a *Metro*. I enjoy the cartoons in the *Metro*. And the photographs of pop stars on marches. All of them. Hundreds of pop stars walking hundreds and hundreds of miles. All the way through the fields of East Scotland.

Politicians have immense respect for pop stars that walk hundreds and hundreds of miles through fields in East Scotland. Their eyes light up when they see one.

There are seventy-two unread messages in my inbox. Nearly all of them relate to the Triford report.

David hasn't slept, he says. He was working on a polish. On two polishes actually. He completed one polish at about eight thirty. He went out for a Chinese meal and afterwards instead of going home he came back and worked all night on another polish. That makes two polishes in one night. The polish is the key stage, he tells me. The polish and the R&D are the key stages of any report. He asks me to print off a copy of the conclusion. I print it off on the wrong type of paper. I print it off on photographic paper. There's photographic paper in the machine and I don't check and he roars at me. Don't I realise what I've done? Don't I realise how much more difficult it is to shred photographic paper? Why didn't I check? Wasn't I thinking? Don't I think? Don't I ever fucking think?

In the afternoon it's like David has been for a shower somewhere. Maybe over his lunch break he went for a swim and got himself a shower after his swim. He doesn't talk to me. I tell him I'm sorry. He says well. You know. There are some people for whom this report means something and some people for whom it clearly doesn't mean so much. He asks me what time I'm working until tonight. I tell him I'll be there until nine. Maybe ten. He doesn't think he'll make it that long. He needs to crash he says. His work is done.

He leaves at six thirty.

Jonathan's picking Lenny up from Julia's tonight because I have to stay late because of the report. I'm on my own. In the office I'm on my own. I recheck the report. I run the figures another time. I double-check the statistics. I become indescribably bored. David has a photograph of himself on his desk. This is surprising to me. I look for jokes on Yahoo. There are images of Sebastian Coe who is getting ready for the announcement in Tokyo tomorrow. All of the people there will wear the same coloured jackets, it says.

I take the report from David's desk. It's nine thirty at night.
It's a Tuesday night. There's nobody else in the office. Maybe
there's nobody else in the whole building. Maybe tonight
there's nobody else in the whole city. I turn on the photocopier.
Warming Up. Please Wait. I turn each page individually face
down onto the glass. I go to the fax machine. I find the
number for Catigar Jones. Fax/Start. Set.

At midday the next day, I went to see what had happened.
And the BBC website said London. For about three minutes
I couldn't believe it. I had to check it and check it and recheck
it again.

Are you laughing or crying?
What?
I said are you laughing or are you crying?

I don't go in on Thursday. They don't want me to go in on
Thursday.

I was the only person in the office on Tuesday night.

I won't take Lenny to see Julia today.

I pick him up and bring him into bed with me. I tickle his
tummy. I blow raspberries on his tummy. What did he need
paint for? I daren't ask him where he goes for his lunch breaks.
Who is he on the phone to on his lunch breaks?

I can feel his ribs underneath his tummy and he's giggling and
when he giggles his legs kick up into the air.

I look into his eyes and he looks right at me. Like he knows
I was the only person in the office on Tuesday night and he
finds it immensely, immensely funny.

The radio's on. Somebody's calling into a phone-in show. He's
just been woken up by a friend of his phoning him from just
south of Russell Square. There's a bus in Russell Square, he
said.

Images of hell.
They are silent.

Six

I wasn't born here. They tell me I was born here, it's not true.

'What the fuck are you talking about, Jason, eh? What the fuck are you like?'

I'm Italian, I'm half Italian. How can I be half Italian if I was born around here?

My mum and dad live here. They live in this house. They've got one room. My sister's twenty-three. She's got one room. I've got one room.

They're completely the same to me. They have exactly the same skin and exactly the same structure of their face. And exactly the same hairstyles. Their clothes are exactly the same. I can't even tell the fucking difference between them half the time.

Dad comes home. Mum's watching the television.

What have you been doing?
You what?
While I've been at work all day. What have you been doing?
I cleaned the house.
You did what?
I cleaned the house. The house. I cleaned it.
Did you?
I did as it goes.
It doesn't fucking look fucking clean.
You what?
I said it doesn't fucking look fucking clean.

Every day.

I don't even like them.

I don't act like them.

You should have seen my sister at school. And I get there and everybody tells me that they taught my sister.

I bet you did.

I'm sorry, Jason?
I said I bet you fucking did.

Sometimes I go into her bedroom and I lie under her bed.

One time she came in. She didn't know I was there. She
moved around. She took something from out of a drawer.
Closed the drawer. Left the room. My heart was beating so
loudly I could feel the blood pressure in my ears.

I got out from under her bed. I got to the drawer that she
opened. Ran my hand through her clothes.

I picked up a stick of lipstick. It was a dull, pink lipstick. I lifted
it to my nose. Smelt it. I opened it up. Licked it a little bit. I put
some on. I was preparing in some ways. I was getting myself
ready in a lot of ways.

The first time I saw her in school I didn't really notice her.
That's quite funny. If you were to say to me, the first time you
saw her in school you didn't notice her. Or the first time you
see her you won't notice her. I'd look at you – I'd give you my
look like –

I don't like it. The school. It's not a good school. Don't believe
anybody who tells you that as schools go it's not a bad school.
Because that's a lie. And we have enough lies in the world,
I think.

The rules here are the rules of the insane.

Don't walk on the left-hand side.
Don't chew gum.
Don't drink water in the corridor.
Don't go to the toilet.
Tuck your shirt in.
Don't stand up.
Unless in Assembly.
Then don't sit down. Ever.

The teachers stand in front of a class and they can't control it.
They stand there. Their eyes going this way and that way.

Their arms flapping about. They can't control their eyes. They can't control their arms let alone a −

Will you be quiet please?
I asked you to be quiet.
I won't ask you again.
I'm going to count to five and if you're not quiet.
One. Two. Three. Four. Five.

On the days when she wears a grey skirt it's like everything has come together at once. Did you ever get a day like that?

I found out that her name was Lisa. I wrote it down.

I wanted to do a BTEC in computers. I don't suppose I'll get the chance now.

There are things wrong with this world. I think when you look at the power that Pakistani people have. And the money they make. There are black people up London and they have meat cleavers. They'll properly kill you. There are Gypsies out by Goresbrook. They take your bike. You'll be going past them on your bike and they'll stop you and they'll say to you − get off your bike. Give it to us. Give us your phone. Give us your trainers. Say you have a nice pair of trainers. Say you saved up or your mum saved up and bought you a nice pair of trainers. They'll just take it. I don't think that's right. Don't tell me you think that's right because it's not.

And white people. The white people round here are left with nothing to do. The women wear clothes that only have one real purpose really. I am part of an Aryan race. I came out of nowhere. It didn't used to be like this. Why do you think it's like this now?

I ask her. Why do you think it's like this now?
She gives me a smile that I swear I've never seen before on any other human being and she says to me, 'I have no idea Jason, you tell me.'

I'm going through the Heathway and I only see one of them at first. He walks towards me.
Aright, Jason?

Pushes into me. Pushes me around.
And before I notice it there's been another one comes up
behind me.
You stood on my toe.
I didn't.
You stood on my fucking toe, you fucking retard cunt.
I didn't mean to. It was an accident. I –
Are you calling me a liar?
Are you calling him a liar, Jason?
Don't call him a liar.
There's a third.
I'd cut his face off if I was you.

I think one of them has a screwdriver.

I'm running across the Heathway into the mall there.
I don't turn round to see where they are.
There's a railing on the side of the Heathway and it slows me
down and they catch me.
And they push me to the ground.
And one of them stamps on my face. He holds my face there
with his foot.
The other has a screwdriver pressed against my cheek.
You fucking pikey thick fucking cunt. You are dead. You call
me a liar. You are so fucking dead.
Don't. Don't. Please don't. Please don't. Don't. Don't.

What happened to your face?

There's blood on my face.
On my shirt. On the pavement. I go into the toilets of the
shopping mall and wash it off.

I don't tell my mum anything.
I don't tell my dad anything.
I don't tell my sister anything.
I have my tea like nothing happened.

I used to deserve this.
I used to be really mouthy in class.
I have the capacity to be really horrible to people.
I have been really horrible to people.

I have been horrible to people about their mothers.
I'm not any more.
This kind of thing used to happen to me all the time.
I don't deserve it any more.

There are ways of smoking cigarettes that I've experimented
with. You can smoke a cigarette like this. Or you can smoke a
cigarette like this. You can light a match like this. Or like this.
Or like this. If you're smoking draw, which is another name
for marijuana, then you should probably smoke it like this.

Lisa smokes Marlboro Lights. Which is about as fucking
obvious as you could ever get.

I go downstairs and my sister's watching Coldplay. They're
singing that song about looking at the stars. I want to kick the
television screen in. Sometimes you think about kicking things
in like that. Stomp on his teeth.

When's Snoop Dog on?
Half five.
You gonna watch him? You gonna watch him? You watching
Snoop Dog?

She says nothing. I go out.

I found Lisa's name in the phone book. I found her address in
the phone book. You wouldn't have thought it would be so
easy, would you? I go to her house. I stand outside her house.
There's nobody there. Nobody's home. Nobody comes in.
Nobody goes out. There's a pub on her corner and they've got
the concert on while I'm waiting.

Madonna brings this coon onstage with her.

Are you ready, London? Are you ready to start a revolution?
Are you ready to change history?

I go back the next day and the house is still empty. Maybe
she's gone away for the weekend. Maybe she's gone to see
some relatives or something like that. I have a cigarette while
I'm waiting. I keep a packet of ten cigarettes in the lining of
my blazer. After a bit I go right up to her window. I wonder
which of these rooms her bedroom is. I can only see the front

room. I imagine her in her front room. Watching the television.
With the curtain closed. I could come round. Watch the
television with her.

Miss.
Yes, Jason?
How are you today?
I'm good thank you, Jason. How are you?
I'm all right. Did you watch *Live 8*?
I watched bits of it.
Did you enjoy it?
I did, yes.
Who did you enjoy best?
I don't know.
Did you like Snoop Dog?
I didn't see him.
Do you think we'll get the Olympics, Miss?
I'm not sure. I think Paris might get it.
It'd be better there, don't you think?
I don't know.
I think it would. It would be better in Paris than in London.
London stinks, I reckon. Don't you think, Miss? Don't you
think London stinks? I think it does. I think it stinks. I think it
stinks of dead people.

Monday night. I get home. I think Dad's started hitting Mum.
I'm not sure. There are bruises across her face. I ask her. She
tells me not to be so ridiculous.

Tuesday morning. Lisa's wearing a red blouse and a grey skirt.
Her hair has come loose at the end of the day. She asks me if
she can get past. I let her pass. She's being rude to me. I think
she's being rude to me. Why's she being rude to me today?
How come she's started being rude to me?

And later she starts talking to the head of maths. It makes me
want to cut his throat open.

Next day. Next maths lesson. This is hilarious. I won't stop
talking. He sends me out. I won't move.

You can't make me.

You can't make me move.
You can't touch me.
You touch me and I'm going to the police.
Sir, you touch me and I'm going to the police.
Sir, do you fancy Miss Watson?
Sir, do you know where she lives? She lives on Parsloes Avenue, doesn't she? Have you been round there?

I could buy a knife. That wouldn't be difficult. I could buy a gun. I could get really fucking drunk and get myself a gun.

How did you find out where I live? Jason, this is serious.
It's in the phone book, Miss. It's not difficult. Do you want a cigarette?
What are you doing here?
I'm just sitting here.
Can you move please?
You were wrong about the Olympics, Miss.
I was what?
I can't fucking believe it myself. I think they must all be insane. Did you see them? Don't you think they're insane? Don't you think Lord Sebastian Coe is insane, Miss? And David Beckham.
Jason, can you move away from my house please?
Where were you at the weekend, Miss?
Where, what?
Where were you at the weekend? You weren't in all weekend. Did you go away for the weekend?
Jason, get off my wall this instant.
Or what?
If you don't get off my wall this instant then I swear I will call the police.
Are you worried about losing your job?
Am I what?
Because teachers and students aren't really meant to fall in love with each other. I'd look after you though. If you did.
Jason, what on earth are you talking about?

There's a fizzing sound. Sometimes with an ashtray or a wall or something you have to rub and rub the cigarette in. It's not like that this time.

Let me say this. Now. After everything that's happened. I would cut out her cunt with a fork. I would scrape off her tits. I would force a chair leg up her arse until her rectum bled. I would do these things. If I was forced to I would do all of these things. Don't think I wouldn't because I would.

On my way up Oxlow Lane there's this guy. He stares at me like he's seen something in my eyes. He's drunk. I think drunk people are the worst. I didn't know if he was going to hit me or kick me or what. He looked at me as though he recognised something. And then he started smiling.

I get home and I go to my room and I put a CD on. I can't stop thinking about the way it made a fizzing sound. It shouldn't have made a fizzing sound. That was a complete surprise to me.

I'd like to go on a roller coaster. Right now that's what I would like. To go to Chessington or Alton Towers and ride on a roller coaster.

Downstairs I can hear Mum and Dad. I don't go down.

I go into my sister's room. I lie down under her bed.

The phone goes. Please don't answer it. Please don't answer it. Please don't answer it.

I go to bed at eight o'clock. I don't even watch much TV.

In the future people will look at me and they'll know I was right about all this. In the future people will do what I say. I'll be like a Führer. Do you think I'm joking? Do you think this is some kind of a joke?

I watch the TV with my sister all morning. She comes back from the tube station. She can't get to work. The images are from CCTV cameras close by to the scene. They change every thirty seconds. I watch them. I keep thinking something is going to happen. The people keep talking but the images only change every thirty seconds or so. I wonder what it's like down there. I wonder what it smells like. I think about the rats. It's such a hot day that I have to close the curtains to stop the sunlight glaring on the television.

I wish she was on the tube. Lisa. I wish Lisa had had a training day and happened to find herself sitting on a tube bound for the centre of town when a young man with a backpack climbed on.

The way the images move, I think the word is tantalising.

I look at my sister.

Are you laughing or are you crying?
What?
Are you laughing or are you crying?

Images of hell.
They are silent.

Five

Have you got any cigarettes?

I'm sorry?

Have you got a cigarette I could have?

Sure. Here.

Can I have the packet?

What?

Can I have your packet of cigarettes?

No, don't be −

Please.

How long are you staying?

Long enough. Don't worry.

I wasn't worried. Believe me.

You're looking well.

Thank you.

You've lost weight.

I have a bit.

You look rather dashing.

Dashing?

But you need to clean your house.

I know.

What room am I staying in?

In here. You can fold the sofa out.

Can't I sleep in your room?

Fuck off.

You could sleep on the sofa.

—

Put some music on.

What music do you want to hear?

You decide. Have you seen Mum and Dad?

Last month. I went up.

How are they?

They're fantastically well. Dad's taken up jogging. Mum keeps buying things. She's bought an array of electronic goods the like of which I've never even heard of.

Good Lord.

I know. Are you going to go and see them?

I might do. I might not. I might have other things to do. Have you got any booze?

No.

Get some.

Alcoholic.

Now.

*

You wanna know my favourite bit? This always happens. It's always hilarious. You'll see them talking about their loss. Maybe their child has been abducted. Or they lost a lover in a terrorist attack. Or a natural disaster. Or just, you know, in the general course of, of, of, of −

Life.

Of life, precisely. And they always do this! They'll be talking perfectly normally. They'll be talking with real grace and often they'll be, they'll be, it's like they'll be −

Happy?

Happy, yes. But then the thought of their lost one, of their child or their lover or their colleague, hits them like a train. And their voices catch in their throats and they can't carry on. Tears well up in their eyes. And what we do is, we stay with them. Every time. We hold them in our gaze for a good twenty seconds before the cut. It has become a formula. That, for me, is one of the highest achievements of our time.

Do you ever get tired?

And I love the way that certain phrases in our language have become like a kind of intellectual Pepto-Bismol. Language is used to constipate people's thinking. Yob Culture. Binge Drinking. What do these things fucking mean? What do they fucking mean exactly? We're losing all sense of precision. Or accuracy. We're losing all sense of language. And at the same time some of the fundamental rights and fundamental privileges of our culture have been removed from us.

Such as?

Simple joys.

Such as?

The simple joy of beating up your lover. The feeling you get
when you molest your own child. The desire to touch the
physically handicapped. Or a burn victim. Or the blemished.
That recoil you get, instinctively.

–

What?

–

What have I said?

*

How did you sleep?

I slept incredibly well. I slept really deeply. I didn't have a
single dream. I closed my eyes. Opened them up again. Eight
hours had passed. It was fantastic.

Would you like some breakfast?

Yes I would, please.

What would you like?

I have absolutely no idea. Surprise me.

You look like you slept well.

You what?

You look rested.

Thank you.

You look great.

Thank you.

It's really good to see you.

Yeah. You too.

You were absolutely mad last night. But it is.

—

What do you want to do today?

Go out.

Where do you want to go?

*

She was a cleaner at St Pancras, at the train station. She found out she was pregnant. This was a hundred years ago. She came here. She spent all her money on getting a room. Threw herself over the side of the stairs. All the way down into the lobby. I've never seen her. People talk about her all the time. That's why they built the handrail.

How did you find out you could get in?

I was persistent.

It's amazing.

People reckon they've seen Roman soldiers marching through the basement. Or there's the man in Room 10.

Who's that?

There's a man who lurks around the back of one of the rooms here. Room 10. If you approach him he runs away. I've seen him. Loads of people have.

Did he run away from you?

Yeah.

He must be mad then.

—

—

They'll open this up. If the Olympics come here. They're gonna build the extension for the Channel Tunnel here. Join us

all up to Europe. You'll be able to go anywhere. They'll re-
open it. It's mine until then.

*

Keep your eyes open.

I am doing.

Any second.

–

–

–

There!

Wow!

It's for the British Museum. It's not been used for sixty years.

Fucking hell.

I know! They closed it because there was no need of it any
more. With Holborn and Tottenham Court Road.

You can imagine the people.

I know.

Standing there.

–

–

The whole city's haunted. Every street there's something
disused. There are forty tube stations, closed for fifty years.
There are hundreds of pubs. There are hundreds of public
toilets. The railway tracks. The canal system. The street map
is a web of contradiction and complication and between each
one there's a ghost.

–

People disappear here in ways they don't in other cities. People get buried in rooms. They get walled up in cellars. They're dug under the gardens. All of these things happen. What? What's funny? Don't you believe me?

Of course I believe you.

What then?

I'm just happy.

What are you happy about?

Seeing you. You idiot.

*

We didn't watch it.

No.

Any of it.

I know.

I bet it was fucking dreadful.

I would have liked to have seen Pink Floyd.

I would have rather cut my eyes out with a spoon.

I'm extremely drunk.

Me too.

—

—

Where were you?

What?

You never told me. All this time.

I was all over the place.

Tell me where.

No.

Why? Why won't you?

–

Were you all right?

–

Were you?

Not really.

Why not?

–

What happened?

You don't need to know.

I'm sorry.

What for?

I'm sorry you weren't all right. I would have done anything to have stopped you from getting hurt.

–

Come here.

–

You smell nice.

Thank you.

You smell like you. Nobody else smells like you. Why is that?

I have no idea.

*

In Moscow all the black marketeers and prostitutes were evacuated from the city centre to create an archetypal image of the dignity of Soviet communism. In Munich the Israeli wrestling went to the theatre to watch *Fiddler on the Roof*. Moshe Weinberg, their coach, got so drunk with the actors afterwards that when the kidnap started he attacked one of Black September with a fruit knife. In Atlanta they flew the flag of the Confederacy from the roofs of most of the venues. In Barcelona trackside officers carried sub-machine guns. I fucking hope London doesn't get it. It'll rip the heart out of the East End. It'll be a catastrophe.

Shut up.

What?

Shut up. Stop fucking talking.

—

Here.

What?

Feel this.

—

Stop talking and feel this.

Where?

Here.

What about it?

It's soft, isn't it?

*

We shouldn't do this.

I know.

It's against every rule that has ever been written by anybody in the whole history of human culture.

I know.

You're my sister.

I know.

This is.

What?

I can't.

Come on.

I can't.

Please. For me. There. There. It feels good. Doesn't it? Well, doesn't it?

*

Oranges.

Oranges?

Yeah. Or apples. Kiwi fruit, a bit.

I didn't know kiwi fruit *had* a smell.

It's a very subtle smell. You smell of it. Very subtly.

You smell of grass.

Grass like draw grass or grass like freshly cut grass?

Freshly cut grass.

Can I ask you something?

Of course.

Are you all right?

Yeah. I am. I'm fine.

—

You look about fifteen. In a good way. There's something about the light on your face.

Can I tell you something?

Go on.

I've wanted to do that for fucking ages.

Have you?

Years.

God.

I know.

What do we do now?

We could get something to eat. We could watch a video. Have you got any porn? We could watch some porn. I'd quite like to watch some porn, I think.

I don't.

We could download some.

Fuck off.

We could go for a walk. Go to Brick Lane and buy a bagel. Get a bottle of wine from the pub next door. I'll put your jeans on and go next door and get a bottle of wine and bring it back here and lie in bed and drink it with you. We could do that. What? Why are you smiling?

Cos I'm happy.

*

Do they know you watch them, do you think?

I've no idea.

Do they ever watch you?

I don't know.

I wonder if they do.

They might do.

They might turn the lights off and lie in the dark and watch you work.

They might do.

Have you ever spoken to them?

No.

I wonder what they're like.

I bet they're cunts.

Don't say that. They might be lovely. What do you think they'd say?

If what?

If they saw us here.

They'd think you were my girlfriend.

What if they knew?

I don't know.

I am kind of your girlfriend, aren't I? A bit.

Kind of.

—

What did they say? At work?

They didn't say anything.

What did you tell them?

I told them you had food poisoning.

*

If I set you a task to do would you do it?

It depends what it is.

It shouldn't.

Well, it would. Don't push it.

If I set you one you could set me one.

Are you sure?

Absolutely.

I might set you a really terrible one.

I wouldn't care.

Or a really rude one.

That wouldn't matter. That would be good.

Go on then.

Take your top off.

Here?

Yeah.

There.

Drop to the floor.

To the floor?

To the ground. I want you to do some press-ups for me.

You what?

I want you drop to the ground and do ten press-ups for me.

–

Thank you. That was lovely.

My turn now.

*

I'm not telling you.

You have to.

I don't.

We made a deal.

It doesn't count.

Yes it does. Of course it does.

That wasn't what I was talking about.

I don't care. I did my press-ups for you. People watched me. Strangers. You made me. You made those rules up. I make the rules of what I want you to do.

I'll do anything else.

I don't want anything else. I want you to tell me what happened.

No.

What happened to you?

No.

What happened to you?

I'm not –

What fucking happened?

Nothing happened. I went away. I thought things would be better than they were. They weren't. I did some jobs. I got my passport stolen. I came back home.

What kind of jobs?

Normal jobs. Jobs. Jobs for money. It was nothing. It wasn't the jobs. It was the disappointment.

–

–

I don't think I understand you.

No.

—

Come to bed with me.

—

We can fuck all night if you want to. I'm not tired. Are you tired? I'm not tired at all. You could tell me all the things you ever wanted to do with me and we could do them and nobody would ever know. I love you so much it's like my body is bursting out of my skin and all I want is for you to love me in the same way and for it to be like this forever. I know that it won't be.

No.

But that's what I want.

*

I should go to work today.

Don't.

I don't want to. I have to go back. There are things I need to do.

What things?

There's a report we need to finish. By next week. Everybody else'll be working their arses off trying to finish it.

Are you not tired?

I'm all right.

Did you sleep?

I did a bit.

Did you see?

What?

London got the Olympics.

Fucking hell.

I know. The French are apoplectic.

We missed it.

I know.

How did we miss that?

I don't know.

It's awful.

I know.

–

Would you like some coffee?

I would please.

–

–

What would I have to do to stop you from going in?

Don't.

What would I have to promise you?
Nothing you promise me will make any difference.

Wouldn't it?

No.

I'll wait for you.

OK.

I'll stay in all day and watch TV and wait for you to come home.

OK.

I'll have your tea ready for you. I'll cook you something nice. I'll go to the shops and get something nice to cook. I'll get your Pink Floyd records out so you can listen to them to make up for the disappointment because everybody says they were brilliant according to this.

Right. That'd be nice.

Can I ask you something?

Go on.

Are you getting a bit frightened now?

*

I was worried about you. You're really late.

I know.

I was terrified. I tried ringing you but all the mobile phone lines were down.

I know. I'm sorry.

You're safe.

Yeah.

Where were you?

They cancelled all the tubes. I had to walk home.

Fucking hell.

What?

Just fucking hell. Fucking hell. Fucking hell.

–

I thought you were dead.

I wasn't.

No.

It's mad out there. Everybody's walking. All the pubs are packed.

–

You need to go.

–

I'm really sorry. You do.

What are you talking about?

You need to go. You need to leave. You can't stay here any more. This is awful. This is all awful. We have to stop doing this. There are some things which you just can't do and fucking hell did you not see the news at all?

Of course I did.

Did you not see what's going on?

What's that got to do with anything?

I can't do this any more. This is all wrong. It's terrible. What are you even doing here? I look at you and all I can see is your stupid fucking horrible fucking face.

Stop it.

I walked home and the place has been destroyed. And I come home to this. And I can't bear it any more and I want it to stop.

I'll kill myself.

I don't believe you.

*

This isn't the last time I'll see you. I will see you again. We will see each other again.

–

I'll tell Mum and Dad you had to go. That it was good to see you. You asked after them. You wanted to see them and then you had to go.

I don't know what I'm going to do without you.

You'll be – People survive. You'll be all right.

You've completely broken my heart.

There are some things that people don't recover from but sadness is never one of them.

It's not about being sad. It's not that I'm sad. For Christ's sake!

No. Sorry.

How long do you think we should wait?

You what?

Until we see each other again. How long do you think we should leave it?

I have no idea.

How long do you think it'll take?

Hundreds and hundreds and hundreds and hundreds of years.

Yeah.

I think about you all the time.

–

I close my eyes and all I ever see is you and your hair and your face and that's not a healthy thing for anybody.

–

You're my sister.

Yeah.

–

–

Have you got everything?

Yes. I think so.

–

–

If you've left anything where should I send it? Is there an address I could send it to?

Throw it away. Put it on eBay. Keep it.

Images of hell.
They are silent.

Four

It's dark. It's still dark when I leave my house.

I kiss my children goodbye. I kiss my wife. I promise that I'll call her.

There's nobody around.

There's the sound of my feet on the gravel of my driveway. The metal on my front gate is cold to touch. My bag slices into my shoulders.

The bus driver turns his face to the road. He's the only vehicle on the road at this time of the morning. He's the only person here.

A young Bangladeshi boy with a Walkman slumps in the middle of the bus towards the right-hand side. Stares out of the window. His feet are rested on the seat in front of him. I sit on the other side. Behind him. I watch the back of his head. I watch his gentle movements to the sound of his Walkman. I take aim. I release the safety catch. I stare down the barrel, down my arm, rigid, straight. I squeeze. I pick up a copy of the morning *Metro*. I look for my horoscopes. I've always looked for my horoscopes.

As we bore into its heart, though, the traffic thickens. There are more buses. Heavy goods vehicles pack up after midnight deliveries. Rumble away again. Lone drivers with no passengers understand the idea of the car pool. They admire the idea of the car pool. They are determined to get involved in a car pool.

They rub eyes with hands balancing coffee in paper cups. Warning. Contents are extremely hot.

We swing round the turnings of the one-way system. I send psychic signals to the bus driver. Drive through the red lights. Turn right on the left turn only. Drive up and over the pavements. From today, from now on you can do, you have it in you to do whatever it is that you want to do. Here is where the rules end. Today is the day when the law stops working.

I thank the bus driver when I get off the bus. I always thank the bus driver when I get off the bus. He doesn't say anything. He stares out of his windscreen. His eyes don't move at all.

I turn out of and away from Piccadilly Gardens.

I climb up the hill towards the railway station.

I could do with a coffee.

I really need a cup of coffee.

Can I have a cup of coffee please? Thank you. Great. Thanks. Thank you.

All of a sudden, as if by magic, there are people everywhere. Turning away from train platforms. Suited and smart and elegant and crisp. Weary-eyed and bloated. Breakfasting on McDonald's or Breakfast Bars or Honey and Granola. Lugging their laptops. Clicking their heels. Pulling their shirt cuffs. Pressing their phones. They've been working all night on a polish. They've been driven by the R&D. Their attention to detail and their R&D is breathtaking.

We have reserved seats in different carriages.

We don't check that each other is here. We don't need to check that each other is here. We trust one another. We're here.

The train arriving on Platform 5 is the 5.43 for London Euston. Calling at Stockport, Macclesfield, Stoke-on-Trent, Milton Keynes Central and London Euston only.

We will take the train to Stoke and get off at Stoke.

From Stoke we will take a train to Derby and change at Derby.

From Derby we will take a train to King's Cross St Pancras.

At King's Cross St Pancras we will each travel on a different tube line. At King's Cross St Pancras one of us will take a Piccadilly Line to Heathrow. One of us will take a Victoria Line to Brixton. One of us will take a Hammersmith and City Line train to Hammersmith. At King's Cross St Pancras I am going to take a Circle Line train via Liverpool Street. We won't speak. We won't signal with one another. We will not communicate with one another in any way. We will, however, each send one text.

I think the weather is warming up. I think we're going to have a beautiful day today. Today the sun will shine all throughout England.

The luggage racks are spacious. They have space for my backpack. There's plenty of room.

This is the first train. There are only a handful of people on my carriage.

And when the second of our number comes into my carriage and sees me he walks right through the carriage and away from me into a carriage further down the train. And we don't speak. And we don't look at one another. We don't say anything at all.

A man sat across the table from me has removed his tie. He furrows his brow at an early-morning anagram, seven across, eight letters, second letter E. He looks like –

I drink bad black coffee from Upper Crust. I am very much in need of mineral water. There are no almond croissants. I want an almond croissant. Where the fuck are your almond croissants, you fucking bewigged, myopic, prurient, sexless dead?

A man down the carriage from me. A young man. He is dressed smartly. He is handsome. He won't stop picking his nose. He burrows around in his nose, removes something from it and surreptitiously, imagining that nobody can see him, slips it into his mouth. Toys with it between his teeth.

By the sides of the tracks as we pull out of Manchester and Stockport there is a mass of containers. There are corrugated-steel industrial units.

I look into the eyes of the woman sat across the seat from me. I think for a second that she's been crying. She hasn't. It's my imagination.

The sunshine through the window of the train is burning up my arms. I want to take my jacket off. Can I take my jacket off please?

I close my eyes for a time. I can sleep now. I try to sleep.

I wake up and panic about how far we've come. I look out of my window as we pull out of Macclesfield.

I've forgotten to do something. There is definitely something that I've forgotten, I've forgotten, can you help me, is there something that I've forgotten? I think it's a word. Is it a word?

I honestly have no memory of changing trains at Stoke. I must have changed trains at Stoke.

East. Out towards Derby.

Disused Jet garage forecourts sit side by side with double driveways. Here there are food-makers and the food they make is chemical. It fattens the teenage and soaks up the pre-teen. Nine-year-old children all dazzled up in boob tubes and mini-skirts and spangly eyeliner as fat as little pigs stare out of the windows of family estate cars. In the sunshine of mid-morning in the suburbs of the South Midlands heroin has never tasted so good. Internet sex contact pages have never seemed more alluring. Nine hundred television channels have never seemed more urgent. And everybody needs an iPod. And nobody can ever get a *Metro* any more.

If I had the power I would take a bomb to all of this. To every grazing horse and every corrugated-metal shed and every wind-blasted tree and every telephone mast and every graveyard. Wipe it all off the skin of the world. Scratch it away.

The only thing I remember about the station at Derby, as we wait at four different points, staring in four different directions, is the oddness of a unisex hairdresser's being there, at the station. Nobody today is having a haircut.

I climb on the third train. Try to close my eyes again. I daren't.

The land rolls on.

I'd like to listen to some music. I'd very much like to listen to the music of Pink Floyd. There's a woman across the aisle from me. She is dressed in a black business suit. She is wearing black tights. I'd very much like to lie in her bed on a Sunday morning eating oven-heated croissants and listening to the music of Pink Floyd.

The teenage girls in the counter of Boots didn't even check the signature on my card. Five hundred bottles of peroxide for hair dye. Fifty bottles of nail varnish remover. I'm making a movie. I'm the runner on a movie.

I want some chewing gum. I want to read the sports pages of a national newspaper.

We're getting closer now. You can tell it. In the shape of the land here.

Glass and concrete and grey metal tubes pepper platforms, punctured by yellow paint at Luton Airport Parkway. Aeroplanes fly throughout the whole of Europe. Don't forget the tax. Don't forget the air tax. Don't forget the consequence. An array of suburbs all throughout Europe have been re-energised by the possibility of cheap flights. There is a legacy of incremental deep-vein thrombosis and an explosion of ramp attendants. Asian boys from suburbs the whole of Europe over have become ramp attendants. Juggling the matrix snake of the luggage hold. Perfecting the ergonomics of bags on wheels. Their mothers package sandwiches in airtight silver foil. Their sisters spray perfume. Their fathers drive buses that move you from one car park to another. Welcome to England.

London rises. It takes you by surprise. Cut out of the edges of bomb blasts. And a thousand years of fire. This is a city that is always on fire. This is a city that is forever under attack.

Nobody checks my ticket. The ticket guards stare at one another's shoes, giggling

St Pancras Hotel is spectre from another time. The whole of the city looms up and over us through the St Pancras Hotel. A metal stairway and the sweep of elegance. Haunted by women who have walked down the stairwell.

There are things I need to say. There is a sequence of words that I've been told I must say. But I can't remember what order it goes in. I want to phone home. I want to tell my wife to wake up and take our children to school. I want to ask her what order the sequence of words is meant to go in.

There is a panelled walkway from St Pancras to the Underground. There are blue arrows telling me to go this way only. I can't seem to feel the weight of my bag any more and I'm terrified that something has gone wrong. Something has gone wrong here. Something terrible has gone wrong.

I follow the blue lines in that way only.

They apologise for any inconvenience that anything may have caused. There is a constant state of apology for any inconvenience that may have been caused.

They have dug up the floor tiles. They are rebuilding everything. They have no choice but to rebuild everything. When the Olympics get here this place will have the newest floor tiles you'll be able to imagine. All of the newspaper headlines, each after the other after the other, are roaring with delight. They cannot believe what happened yesterday. Nobody can believe what happened yesterday and what that will mean.

I pay £2.20 for a single ticket to Zone 2 via Zone 1 stations.

I smile at the man who holds the gate to the platform open for me so that I can get through with my bag. But he doesn't smile back. He doesn't check my ticket. He doesn't even look at me. He looks away from me.

The second of our number sends me a text message. The third of our number sends me a text message. The first of our number sends me a text message. I reply to them all.

I follow the signs for the Circle Line. The platform is busy. The platform is busier than I expected it to be. I find the space for the busiest carriage. At the heart of the train. I have to push my way on with my bag. People are complaining about the size of my bag.

Suddenly I feel lighter than I have ever felt in my whole life.

We move past Farringdon. Where the platform is open and sunk in the grey blue light of morning. And red-brick Moorgate. Liverpool Street is white with sugar and pace and desire. Smoke blue, blood red, ghost white.

The train pulls out of Liverpool Street and moves towards Aldgate.

Three

You look just like him.

That's not true.

You've got the same eyes. You've got exactly the same hair. How old is he?

He's twenty-five.

He's very handsome.

I worry about him constantly.

What do you worry about?

I worry that he won't achieve the things he has the potential to achieve. I worry that nobody will ever fall in love with him. That he won't get out of bed. Ever. That he'll die before me. Things like that.

Solipsist.

He is incredibly vulnerable. He has absurdly soft skin, for a man of his age. Did you call me a solipsist?

You are.

I'm not in the least bit solipsistic. I'm not a solipsist at all.

You're projecting onto him. Mercilessly.

That's not true. It's the opposite of that.

Would you like another drink?

I'm not sure now.

Are you all grumpy and cross now?

I'm just not sure if I want to be insulted by you.

It's incredibly good to see you.

I was going to say that it's good to see you too. Until you started insulting me.

You're looking fantastic. You funny little man. You've lost weight. Your skin's cleared up.

My skin?

I remember your skin being kind of blotchy. We used to stare at it during your seminars.

Did you?

It isn't now.

Who stared at me?

All of us. It looks fresh now. You look good.

Thank you.

That's my pleasure.

I think I would like another drink. I think I'd like another Merlot.

I bet you would.

Will you buy me another Merlot please?

It's funny, isn't it?

What is?

People's faces. When people get older their faces don't change. They just decay a little bit. The shape is the same, though. The shape of their eyes. You recognise them completely. They send off little messages through your synapses.

Your face has changed. Your eyes have got smaller. How did that happen?

I have no idea. It's the same with voices, by the way. The speed with which we recognise one another's voices when we pick up our telephones is staggering to me. Human beings are so fucking clever that sometimes it makes me want to fall over.

Should I go myself, to get my drink?

Don't you think I'm funny?

No.

I am. I think I am. I make myself laugh my head off. Wait here.

*

I went to America.

Good thinking.

I got myself a job in a faculty in Minneapolis.

What was Minneapolis like?

It was fantastically cold. You go outside in winter and after seconds, literally seconds, your nasal hairs freeze over. That was unusual.

It sounds it.

The students were banal. They all had the same haircut, which disconcerted me. And everybody was fat. You had to walk for twenty minutes to get any fresh fruit. Even then it was coated in genetically modified chemical additive.

How long were you there for?

Two years. I found it difficult to get the energy to leave. I blame the diet.

And how long have you been back?

Four years.

Four years?

Yeah.

Jesus.

What?

When did you graduate?

Eight years ago.

I'm nearly literally twice your age.

Yeah.

That makes me feel terrible. That makes me feel like I'll probably die soon.

You might.

Well, yes. I might. We all might. Anybody might. But I probably will. Is my point.

I enjoyed the teaching.

Did you?

I want to teach again.

–

–

That's where I come in.

No.

No?

I mean maybe. I mean yes. Really I mean yes.

You don't sound like you enjoyed the teaching.

I did. I just didn't enjoy the students. I hankered after British students. I kept imagining how great British students would be.

They're not.

I bet they fucking are. I need a job.

Yeah. We all need a job.

I can't work in bars again. I'm far too old to get a bar job. It would be so humiliating.

You can't even remember to get people drinks.

No.

I'll see what I can do.

–

I'll talk to the Dean. I have no idea if there's anything available.

Thank you.

That's OK.

This is my grateful face. This is my excited face. This is my excited and grateful face.

They're remarkable.

I know. Have you eaten?

What?

Supper. Have you had any supper?

No.

No. Neither have I.

*

It gets to a point in a marriage where the house is full of these horrible psychic forces. You can feel the anger. I'd come into the house and look at her standing in the living room or in our bedroom and there would be part of me that would want to cave her head in with a brick. That's quite an unnerving feeling.

You should have left each other earlier than you did by the sound of things.

There was Mark. I didn't want to leave while he was still living there.

No.

—

—

—

Have you lived round here since?

Yes. I have. I've got a flat. It's got two bedrooms. I don't have a television. Mark comes to see me if he's in town but he never stays the night even though the reason I got the spare room in the first place was for him. Fucking ingrate.

You don't mean that.

No. I enjoy seeing him. I like taking him to the pub and talking to him about work and about football as though we were mates. I talk to him about his mum. Make sure she's all right.

Is she?

She's having a ball. She's living with the father of one of
Mark's school friends. A gentle, decent, intelligent man who
I still occasionally bump into and who, despite my best
intentions to the contrary, I can't bring myself to dislike.

Cunt.

I know.

—

—

Do you like living on your own?

I do. You know? I do. I do. I do. I really do. I like shopping for
food. I like discovering food shops in odd places and going
there. I like eating out occasionally on my own. Going to the
cinema and not worrying about being back in time. Going to
the pub and staying there. Working all night if I want to.
Naked. At my desk. Scratching my balls.

Lovely.

I know. And I've started running.

Have you?

I've taken up jogging.

I thought you'd lost weight.

I love it. Round the park. I did four laps on Saturday. I'm
going to enter the Olympics, I think.

You should.

I will.

—

What do you think that'll be like?

What?

The Olympics.

I have no idea.

Don't you think it'll be rather brilliant?

I'm not sure.

I was in my car this afternoon, when they announced it. I had the radio on. And the hosts of the Olympic Games in 2012 will be . . . London! I punched my fists in the air. I nearly punched the roof off the car. I honked my horn in celebration. Other people did too. It was like we were having a big party on the road, in our cars. Everybody was grinning at each other.

I didn't really know what to think.

Oh come on! You know? Life is so short.

*

Are you not cold?

No.

Would you like to borrow my scarf?

–

What?

Nothing.

–

I used to come here when I was a child. To the museum. Have you ever been in there?

No.

You should go in. There are dolls in there from four hundred years ago. Other dolls, porcelain dolls from the nineteenth century with three faces. They're terrifying. I'll take you.

Will you?

You get me a job and I'll bring you to the museum and show you the dolls with the three faces.

Would you like some coffee?

I'm sorry?

Would you like to come in and have a cup of coffee with me?

*

It's from Jamaica.

Right.

From Blue Mountain. It's the most exclusive coffee in the world. How do you like that?

Very flash.

What do you think?

It's lovely. Thank you.

Good. Good. I'm glad.

I like your flat.

Do you?

I do. It's simple. It's spare. It's minimalist.

There's nothing here, you mean.

It feels deliberate.

It isn't.

That's not the point. I like the view. You can see the Gherkin.

Yes. I rather like that. Would you like to stay?

I'm sorry?

Here. Tonight.

—

I don't mean to 'stay' stay. I mean. I've got the room. And it's late. It'd be difficult for you to get back now. You'd have to get the night bus. And the night bus from here is like one of the lower circles of hell. You'd never survive it.

—

I'd make you breakfast.

—

It's been very good to see you. I'm sorry. I shouldn't have asked.

—

—

You had no idea, of course, at the time. But you were everything to me. You were my teacher. I was completely besotted with you. I wanted you, what I wanted you to do was, I wanted you to notice me. Of course you never did. You shouldn't have asked me. No. You probably really shouldn't.

*

The sheets are completely untouched. They're practically brand new.

Thank you.

Have you got some pyjamas?

Pyjamas?

You can borrow some. If you need to. I've got piles and piles of the things.

Thank you.

What time do you need to get up in the morning?

I don't really need . . . I'm not working at the moment.

I get up absurdly early. I have completely lost the ability to sleep any more. So I'll wake you up at any time you want.

Nine o'clock. How's nine o'clock. Is that all right?

A lie-in!

Kind of.

–

–

It'll be quite funny wearing your pyjamas.

Funny?

I've not worn pyjamas for years. Not since I was a little girl.

–

What?

Can I ask you something?

Of course.

Will you dance with me?

–

If I put some music on. Would you dance with me?

*

Are you crying?

What?

I couldn't tell if you were laughing or if you were crying.

Shhhh.

Hey. Hey. Don't cry.

I'm not.

Hey.

–

–

–

Don't.

Shhhh.

Don't, please.

Shhhhh.

Please don't.

Come on.

–

I can feel you breathing.

Please don't.

You know exactly what you're doing to me. You've known all night what you've been doing to me.

–

What knickers are you wearing? Tell me.

Be quiet.

Are you even wearing any?

Christ.

Come on. I'm noticing you. This is me noticing you.

–

Ow.

–

Ow. You fucking. You. That fucking hurt.

–

I should beat the crap out of you for doing that.

–

Don't tell me that you didn't want exactly what –

Is there a lock on that door?

What?

Is there a lock on the bedroom door?

–

Can it be locked from the inside?

Yes. Of course it can.

I need to sleep somewhere.

–

–

–

You're quite little, aren't you?

Little?

I've never noticed before.

*

I'm very sorry. For what I did last night. I was awful.

It's not enough.

No. Of course not.

–

I made you some breakfast. I cooked bacon and everything.
Will you stay for breakfast? Will you stay for breakfast, please?

–

–

I need to get to Edgware Road. Can I get the train to Edgware
Road from near here?

I dreamt about you last night. It was horrible. The dream was horrible.

—

I woke up. I thought my wife was there. I thought she was sleeping next to me. She looks like Mark when she's asleep. She wasn't. I was on my own. I'm fucking cracking up is the thing. I'm completely losing my fucking mind.

—

These things, they're not bruises. They don't fade. They're scars.

Two

You never get bus conductors any more. On some tube lines now you don't even get drivers. The machines have started to run themselves.

I like this.

I have absolutely no interest in speaking to anybody.

In the free newspaper there is talk of the events of the weekend. They write, in this paper, without any editorial bias. I hate the fucking thing. They've removed any semblance of perspective or personality.

This was not music. What they did on Saturday was the opposite of music. It was everything I wish I had the strength to rip down and destroy. I'd take a pickaxe to the lot of them. They manifest charity masquerading as action. They are driven by a singular spirit of self-congratulation. It makes me want to bite the throats out of their domestic pets.

I have an article to deliver.

I take the bus to the entrance of the faculty. Walk up Gower Street. The university brackets the road with the hospital. Right through the northern heart of central London. One starts in one bracket. Crosses. Returns.

I haven't worked there, properly, for fifteen years now. They look at me with a mix of bewilderment, pity and an odd kind of rage. I leave my article for Dr Schults. He'll call me.

I go back home.

There was a time when I'd walk. Gower Street to Hammersmith.

I couldn't do it any more. I can barely fucking breathe half the time.

Wait for the bus. Get the bus. Get home. Drink tea. Try not to spend too many hours staring out of the window. If you stare long enough into a mirror, of course, you begin to hallucinate. My entire life has the feeling of that nowadays.

I watch television with a mixture of awe and horror.

Sometimes I forget if I've eaten or not. It is as likely that this will lead to me eating two meals of an evening as it is that I'll end up eating none. I wouldn't be at all surprised if I became enormously fat.

I don't see anybody. I don't speak to anybody. And God, the fucking horror if I were forced to. I wouldn't know what to do with my hands. Occasionally letters are delivered. Letters from abroad that may require a signature. I go to the door. I swear that they can see it in my eyes. The blank shivering terror.

Where do I sign?

Do you need a date with that?

Do you need the time of delivery to be recorded?

Would you like to come in for a cup of tea?

There are few things that have caused me more pleasure in recent years than the coverage of the war in Iraq. This offers me the same kind of thrills as do exciting video games. There was a time when I played video games quite often. The feeling I get watching war coverage is the same.

In the evenings I wear my husband's robe. Most of his clothes were wrapped by his sister into black bin liners and taken away to a variety of shops. His robe was saved. I pull the blinds down. And I turn the computer on. Sometimes I don't pull the blinds down. Sometimes I like the idea that in the middle of the night, in the heart of west London, all of the neighbours can see me. His gown is, it's this red, silk gown. I let my hand fall beneath it.

I watch the trailers. Every trailer follows a genre convention. There's a moment, at the end of every film, where the girl is waiting for the boy to come. Kneeling below him. Looking up. She asks him to come on her face. And at that moment she looks tired and worn out and the good years, when the work was flying in, have taken their toll. And you do kind of think.

Dr Schults doesn't ring me. He doesn't ring me to tell me he got the article. He doesn't email. He doesn't acknowledge it in any way.

I lose complete track of when I go to bed.

I have the same thing for breakfast every day. I have a hundred grams of muesli mixed with fifty grams of fresh berries and milk and honey and yogurt. I have some fresh orange juice and some coffee. And then I go up to my desk and I start to work.

And in between jobs. When an article is finished and there are no new commissions waiting to begin I can sit at my screen and I simply have no idea what to do. And the pull, my God, the pull towards the world that is there, on the other side of my screen!

I have to leave in the end. To go shopping. To buy ingredients to make some food. To go into town. To go to a museum. To do anything I possibly can to get away from my computer.

I hate shopping for my own food. I see other people in food shops and they fill me with the deadness of real despair. What is the point of buying aubergines when there are people in the world who dress like that? And who have faces like that? And talk with accents like that? And treat their children like that?

In town everybody's talking about the possibility that the
Olympic Games might be coming to London. I'm struck by
the irony of this. Because the people of London, palpably to
me, are universally obese and under-exercised. Fat fuckers.
Gibbering about athletes. The lot of them.

London in summer is a horror story. The Underground is a
cauldron. The shopping centres are brutalised. There is no
such thing as air conditioning.

She's dressed in a baby-doll nightie. With a red eye mask over
the top of her face. And she asks him if he's her daddy. Call
me Daddy. Will you call me Daddy? And it doesn't bother me.
It doesn't matter to me how old she is.

Two days pass like this.

There are images of things that I have seen seared onto the
inside of my skull.

And then on Wednesday lunchtime the news comes in that
London's bid to host the Olympics in 2012 has been successful.
And now people smile. Transistor radios broadcast the events
over and over. We go live to Trafalgar Square. We go live to
Tokyo where Lord Coe is speaking. We go live to the derelict
battered crack dens of Stratford where residents there can
barely contain their glee at the prospect of Kelly Holmes
racing madly around the peripheries of their houses.

Cars do little dances. Drivers toot their horns at one another
with idiot inane grins on their faces. Shocked by their own
daring. Epileptic with thoughts of how old they'll be in 2012.

And when I get back Dr Shults has called. He's left a message
for me on my phone. This is BT Call Minder 1571. The
person you are calling is not available. Please leave a message
after the tone.

I listen to the message three times. Put some music on. Pour
myself a whisky. Pour myself another. I smoke an entire packet
of cigarettes in one sitting.

What I realise now is that I won't die. I'm going to live on and on.

He wants me to see him the next day. He wants me to go in and see him the next morning to talk about things.

I don't sleep.

At three o'clock in the morning I go outside into the garden. This city is never silent. At this time of morning it hums and roars in the distance. It has a throb and a pulse of its own. It feels latent. It feels charged. It feels sprung. As though something remarkable is going to happen.

I go back to bed eventually. I have no idea what time it is.

I am eighty-three years old next month.

I get up. Measure out my breakfast. Get dressed. Get on the tube. Go and see Daniel.

But it's clear by the time I get to the tube station that something is going wrong. Nobody says anything. But Hammersmith tube station is closed. Both stations actually. For all three lines. On each side of the roundabout.

The traffic into town has stopped completely still.

Posters warn me not to make any journeys unless they're completely necessary.

I walk.

I walk through Hammersmith up towards Shepherd's Bush. Up Holland Park Road on to Notting Hill Gate. Down Notting Hill Gate up to the corner of the park. Down Oxford Street to Tottenham Court Road. Up Tottenham Court Road towards Gower Street. I'm very late. There's nobody there. Nobody came in today. Nobody at all came into the centre of London today. Nobody rang to let me know.

On my way back my feet, I think, start to blister and it feels like they might start bleeding.

There are masses of people waiting at bus stops. I see one man. He does look like my husband. Just for a second I was thrown. But he's far too young. He can't be more than forty. Did he see me looking at him? Did I frighten him? Did I frighten you? Were you frightened? I didn't mean to frighten you.

It's on days like this that I realise how intelligent my decision to talk you out of having children was. I mean, can you imagine? Really. Can you imagine what would have happened?

And tonight, I think, everybody in London walked home.

It's getting dark by the time I get back. As I approach my house the streets get smaller and they are quieter. I can't feel my feet any more. I think my socks have stuck to the soles of my feet.

It's a warm evening. There is the noise of music coming from one of the houses. People are listening to music of some description. And somebody close by is having a barbecue.

I can smell chicken. I can smell barbecued chicken cooking. It smells good.

It's nine o'clock.

I find the house where the chicken is being cooked and I knock on the door.

Hello.

– Can I help you?

I, I, I'm sorry.

– Can I, is there anything – ?

I walked past your house. I could smell chicken.

– What?

It smells delicious.

– We're having a barbecue. I'm sorry. Can I help you?

Can I have some?

– Can you – ?

I just wanted you to know that I think your chicken smells delicious.

– Thank you. You said.

And I wondered what would happen if I just knocked on your door and said, your chicken smells delicious, please can I have some of it?

– Ha.

Don't laugh.

– That's quite funny to me.

Don't laugh at me.

– How old are you?

What?

– You're completely fucking retarded, sweetheart, aren't you?

Don't laugh at me.

– Here.

What?

– Wait here. Don't come in.

–

–

–

–

–

–

–

– Here.

Thank you.

– I don't have any napkins. I'm sorry.

No. No. No. No. This is fine. This is kind of you. This is lovely. Thank you.

– I'd have brought you a beer but I decided not to.

No. I don't want a beer. I just wanted some chicken. I just wanted – This is lovely. Thank you.

I walk home. The chicken tastes good. I let myself in. I can't feel my feet any more. I can't understand why there are tears pouring down the sides of my face. This makes absolutely no sense to me at all.

On the evening of 7 July 2005 many of the working people of London walk home from their workplaces in the centre of the city.

Images of hell.
They are silent.

One

1 A church deacon, he was a man known for his deeply held Christian faith and tolerance of other religions.

2 She usually drove to her PA job while her boyfriend preferred to cycle from their home in Tottenham, north London.

3 He had just moved in with his boyfriend of three years but also spent much of his time looking after his widowed mother, who suffers from multiple sclerosis.

4 Her daughter had just arrived in London from Poland on the day her mother was killed.

5 He was passionate about two things: his family and sport.

6   If he was known for anything, it was for his sense of fun.
    If there was a party to go to or on occasion to celebrate,
    he would always be the first and the loudest there.

7   Even in this time of sadness, friends tend to laugh when
    discussing his life. It happens when they talk of his
    passionate defence of all things Arsenal, should anyone
    have dared mock his much-loved football club.

8   She came to Britain five years ago from Mauritius.

9   One of three sisters from a distinguished Italian family,
    she was preparing for a great celebration in Rome which
    would have united Catholic and Muslim rites.

10 She was making her daily journey to University College
    London Hospital where she worked as an administrator
    in the neuroradiology department when she boarded the
    Piccadilly line train on 7 July.

11 He was on his way to the Royal Borough of Kensington
    and Chelsea, where he worked as a human resources
    systems development officer.

12 He was on his way to a one-day course at the Kensington
    branch of Jessops, the camera chain. He sent a text
    message to his mother twenty-one minutes before the first
    blast, and that was the last his parents heard from him.

13 The twenty-six-year-old, an engineering executive from
    Hendon, was killed on the number 30 bus after he was
    evacuated from King's Cross.

14 His hit calypso is still played on local radio station ZJB,
    many years after it was recorded. But calypso was merely
    his hobby, albeit a highly acclaimed one.

15 When he was a teenager, his father caught him putting on
    his sister's heavy black mascara. He was going through a
    goth phase and had dyed his hair to match.

16 She was due to leave London on the evening of 7 July for
    a romantic long weekend in Paris with her boyfriend. The

day before she died, her dad was wallpapering the kitchen, and she scrawled the words '06/07/05 we got the Olympic bid 2012 on this day' on the bare wall.

17 His hobbies included waterskiing, quad-bike riding and skiing. He had a lifelong love of music and met his fiancée, seven years ago, in a rock club.

18 He helped to set up the Ipswich and East Suffolk hockey club nine years ago.

19 She had taken leave from her job with a Turkish textile company to improve her English.

20 He was former chairman of the Polish Solidarity Campaign of Great Britain, vice chairman of the Havering branch of the Humanist Society, chairman of the H.G. Wells Society and a long-standing supporter of the Anti-Slavery Society among other charities.

21 She had just sent text messages to friends telling them she had safely been evacuated from the tube. As well as travelling and socialising she loved music, and recently went to see Coldplay in Thailand.

22 She worked for BBC Books and the *Sun* for a short time.

23 She had lived in Luton for twenty-five years.

24 She attended the mosque every Friday, but loved Western culture and fashions and regularly shopped for designer clothes, shoes and handbags. She worked as a cashier at the Co-operative Bank in Islington.

25 She was evacuated from the Underground at Euston and decided to catch a bus to work.

26 Deciding that university was not for her, she moved to Salamanca for a year to learn Spanish. Her first job was in the wine trade, which took her abroad again, to Australia, where she lived in Melbourne for a year.

27 He travelled all over Europe as a product technical manager for the clothes manufacturers Burberry.

28   She had a successful career as an accountant in Glasgow
      and later the City, but she was as happy helping out at
      homeless hostels as she was discussing the financing of
      management buyouts.

29   Her taxi-driver husband described her as a 'devoted and
      much-loved wife and mother of two sons'.

30   He survived fleeing Vietnam as one of the boat people
      when he was less than a year old.

31   She was born in Auckland, New Zealand.

32   He was born in Vietnam, the son of a South Vietnamese
      soldier killed in the conflict when he was just five months
      old.

33   On a normal day, a politics graduate from Warwick
      University, he would have used a completely different
      route to his place of work.

34   There, on a website he helped create, hundreds of people
      have posted almost 18,000 words of tribute.

35   She was born in Tehran but made her home in London
      twenty years ago.

36   One of the last tasks she completed, with her usual
      cheerful verve, was promoting a new rose at Hampton
      Court flower show, named in honour of the Brownies on
      their ninetieth anniversary.

37   She was an optimist. Her mother is certain she would have
      taken comfort in the compassion and caring shown to her
      family over the past fortnight.

38   She had lived in London for eighteen years and was
      nervous about visiting her native Israel because of the risk
      of suicide bus bombings.

39   She missed London; the people, the lifestyle, the pubs. So,
      after completing a two-year dental technology degree at
      the Los Angeles City College, she turned down an offer to
      continue her studies at the prestigious UCLA and returned
      to her adopted home town.

40 On any given Thursday night, she could be found at
    Chiquito in Staples Corner, the Mexican restaurant of
    choice for nights out with her friends Nell Raut and
    Andrea Cummings.

41 He was the kind of man people went to with their problems.
    'He always had time to listen,' said his father.

42 His parents were killed by the Taliban when he was a
    teenager. He left his family in Afghanistan and arrived in
    Britain in January 2002 and was granted exceptional leave
    to stay. He was the only Afghan national to be killed in the
    bombings, and the last of the victims to be formally
    identified.

43 –

44 When he went on a three-month trip around Ghana,
    Senegal and Mali last year, he was satisfying a long-held
    ambition.

45 In 2003, she joined the specialist criminal law firm
    Reynolds Dawson as an assistant solicitor and worked as
    a duty solicitor in court and police stations, specialising in
    fraud and extradition.

46 She came to London earlier this summer to get a taste of
    big city life.

47 She was full of high hopes when she gave her mother her
    usual goodbye kiss at Liverpool Street. Mother and daughter
    always caught the same train from Billericay and had
    developed the fond little ritual as they went their separate
    ways. Ms Taylor had just heard that her temporary contract
    as a finance officer at the Royal Society of Arts in the
    Strand had been made permanent.

48 She dedicated her life to helping children as a radiographer.

49 She was a personal assistant who lived with her partner in
    Islington, north London.

50 Coming to Britain from Ghana in the mid-1980s was
    almost an accident for her. The Lebanese bank manager

she worked for in her home town was forced to move to London for his son's medical treatment and Mrs Wyndowa travelled with him to care for the family. When they returned to Lebanon, she remained in the UK, where she had made a new life.

51   He followed the same routine on the way to work every day for ten years. After leaving home shortly before 8 a.m., the IT specialist would take the tube to Liverpool Street, where he would join the early-morning regulars at Leonidas Belgian chocolate shop for a double espresso at 8.30 a.m. After half an hour quietly listening to others holding forth he would make the short walk to the offices of Equitas Holdings in St Mary Axe, where he worked.

52   Determined to improve his English, he headed for London shortly after gaining an IT engineering degree from the University Institute of Technology (IUT) in Saint-Martin-d'Hères, near Grenoble. He shared a flat in Kensal Green with three friends and worked in a pizza takeaway. He sent any spare money home to his younger sister but managed to save enough from his modest wages to buy a computer.